Financial Freedom

Strategies for Budgeting, Saving, Investing, and Building Wealth

Isaac Wilson

Table of Contents

Introduction

In a world when having stable finances can seem like an unattainable goal, the idea of financial freedom has promise. Achieving financial freedom entails more than just possessing a substantial amount of money; it also involves managing your finances, living your life as you see fit, and finding peace of mind despite changes in the economy. In addition to giving readers a summary of what to expect from this book, this introduction delves into the importance of financial freedom.

Comprehending the Significance of Financial Independence

For many people who aspire to be independent and feel secure in their lives, financial independence is the ultimate objective. It represents freedom from debt restrictions, reliance on income from a job, and anxiety about money. Those who achieve financial freedom are better able to follow their passions, see the globe, donate to causes they care about, and live comfortably in retirement.

Additionally, a sense of happiness and tranquilly comes along with financial freedom. The security that comes with having a solid financial foundation protects against unforeseen costs, job loss, and downturns in the economy. Knowing they have the means to get through difficult times enables people to face financial storms with fortitude and assurance.

Overview of the book's main points

This book is intended to serve as a thorough guide for readers as they set out on their path to financial independence. It addresses a number of personal finance topics, such as wealth-building techniques, investing, saving, and budgeting. Every chapter is designed to provide readers the tools they need to take charge of their financial future by offering useful information, doable solutions, and practical insights.

Essential financial principles, such the value of budgeting, the effect of compound interest, and the several investment vehicles that can be used to increase wealth, are taught to readers throughout the book. Along with learning how to overcome typical financial roadblocks like debt, they will also learn how to create a strong financial foundation that can weather economic downturns.

In general, this book seeks to give readers the information, abilities, and mindset required to attain financial independence and lead fulfilling lives. Readers can embark on a revolutionary journey towards wealth and financial freedom by adhering to the concepts contained in these pages.

Chapter 1: Foundations of Financial Freedom

Anyone may attain financial freedom with the correct attitude and money management strategy; it's no longer just a pipe dream. We'll discuss the fundamentals of financial independence in this chapter, including what it means to be financially free and how to define and set realistic financial objectives for yourself.

Definitions of Wealth and Financial Freedom

Many times, people mistakenly believe that being financially free means only having a lot of money or being able to live a lavish lifestyle. True financial independence, on the other hand, isn't only about having a lot of money; it's also about being able to make decisions on your own terms, without having to worry about how your money is being spent. To be financially free means to be able to pay for your bills, follow your interests, and deal with financial setbacks without being overly anxious or stressed.

Contrarily, wealth is more than just material prosperity. Wealth encompasses both tangible and intangible assets, such as relationships, personal fulfilment, and health, in addition to tangible assets like money, investments, and property. Having abundance outside of your bank account is what defines true prosperity.

Determining Individual Financial Objectives

Establishing your own financial objectives is crucial before starting the path to financial freedom. Your financial decisions and activities will be guided by these goals, which will also keep you motivated and focused throughout the process. It's critical to define financial goals that are SMART—specific, measurable, realistic, relevant, and time-bound. This guarantees that your objectives are distinct, reachable, and consistent with your overarching future vision.

Some common financial goals may include:

1. Creating an emergency fund to meet unforeseen bills is one typical financial objective.

2. Reducing high-interest debt in order to become financially independent.

3. Setting aside money for immediate objectives like a trip or house makeover.

4. Making investments for future needs like a child's schooling or retirement.

5. Creating sources of passive income to become financially independent.

A road map for reaching financial freedom and gradually accumulating wealth can be created by outlining your financial objectives in detail and ranking them according to significance and urgency. The important thing is to remain dedicated to your financial path and take consistent action towards your goals, no matter how big or small.

In conclusion, knowing what it really means to be wealthy and financially free, as well as establishing specific, SMART financial objectives that are in line with your beliefs and aspirations, are the cornerstones of financial freedom. These guidelines will help you build a solid foundation so you may start your path to abundance and financial empowerment.

Chapter 2: Budgeting for Success

The foundation of financial success is budgeting. It offers a road map for handling your earnings and outgoings, assisting you in setting spending priorities, making cost reductions, and reaching your financial objectives. This chapter will discuss the value of budgeting and offer doable methods for setting up and sticking to a personal spending plan that suits you.

Establishing and Preserving Your Personal Budget

A personal budget is a financial plan that, usually on a monthly basis, details your income, expenses, and savings objectives for a given time frame. The process of making a budget consists of three key steps: figuring out how much money you make, keeping track of your spending, and dividing it up among several categories including housing, transportation, groceries, and entertainment.

Listing all of your sources of income, such as earnings, salaries, bonuses, and any additional sources of income, is the first step in creating a personal budget. After that, keep tabs on your spending by reading over your bank statements, invoices, and receipts to see where your money is going. Sort your expenditures into two categories: variable (such as groceries and eating out) and fixed (such as rent and utilities).

As soon as your income and costs are clearly visible to you, divide the money among the categories according to your financial objectives and priorities. Make sure your budget accounts for savings goals including an emergency fund, retirement contributions, and other long-term goals.

Keep a regular check on your spending and change your budget as necessary. To simplify the process and maintain organisation, use applications and tools for budgeting. Periodically review your budget to make sure you are adhering to your financial objectives and moving closer to realising them.

Methods for Monitoring Expenses and Controlling Cash Flow

An essential component of creating a budget is keeping track of your expenditures in order to spot potential areas for overspending and discover places where you may cut costs. To successfully track your costs, you can employ a number of strategies:

1. Keep thorough records: Whether you do this digitally with spreadsheets or budgeting tools, or manually in a notebook, keep a record of every penny you spend. No matter how minor the transaction, be sure to meticulously note it.

2. Make use of cash envelopes: Set aside money for several types of expenses and place separate envelopes for each (e.g., groceries, dining out). This makes your expenditures easier to see and helps you avoid overspending in particular areas.

3. Establish spending caps: Decide how much money can be spent on entertainment, eating out, and shopping, among other discretionary costs. To prevent impulsive purchases and stay inside your budget, abide by these restrictions.

4. Automate bill payments: To prevent late fees and guarantee that necessary

expenses are met each month, set up automatic payments for recurring bills like rent, utilities, and subscriptions.

5. Regularly check your spending: Set aside some time each week or month to go over your expenses and make sure they match your budget. Seek out patterns or trends that can point to areas where you might reallocate money or make savings.

Through the application of these techniques and maintaining a strict budgeting regimen, you may improve your money management, lessen stress, and work towards obtaining stability and financial freedom. Budgeting is about empowerment and directing your spending towards your objectives and ideals, not about imposing restrictions.

Chapter 3: The Power of Saving

Achieving financial security and freedom requires saving money. It entails reserving a portion of your income for unforeseen expenses, large expenditures, or long-term financial objectives. We'll discuss the value of saving and how it affects your overall financial health in this chapter.

The Value of Savings for Structural Security

In order to develop resilience and financial security, saving is essential.

Here are some main arguments for the significance of saving:

1. Emergency fund: By setting aside money for unforeseen costs like auto repairs, medical bills, or job loss, you can avoid taking on high-interest debt or using up all of your savings. Your emergency fund should have enough cash to cover three to six months' worth of living expenditures.

2. Financial independence: By acting as a safety net and lowering your reliance on outside income sources, saving helps you attain financial independence and freedom. If you have enough saved up,

you may take career chances, follow your passions, and retire early without worrying about running out of money.

3. Reaching financial objectives: Savings is necessary to reach short- and long-term financial objectives, like property ownership, college funding, or a comfortable retirement. You can increase your wealth and work towards your goals by saving and investing regularly over time.

4. Peace of mind: Financial stress is lessened when you know you have money to fall back on in an emergency. You may concentrate on other facets of your life,

like professional development, personal improvement, and quality time with loved ones, when you are financially secure.

Differing Between Savings Objectives: Short-Term and Long-Term

It's critical to distinguish between short- and long-term savings objectives when it comes to saving and to use your resources appropriately.

1. Short-term savings objectives: These are usually related to costs you anticipate having to pay within the next year or two, such holidays, house repairs, or buying a

new gadget. These objectives can be met by making recurring contributions to a money market fund or savings account, which both require reasonably liquid assets.

2. Long-term savings objectives: These entail making plans for major outlays or life events that are several years or decades off, such home ownership, college funding, or retirement. A more disciplined approach to investing and saving, with contributions to retirement accounts like brokerage accounts, IRAs, and 401(k)s, is frequently necessary to achieve these goals.

Prioritising your financial objectives according to their significance and time span is crucial. Establish an emergency fund first to cover pressing expenses, then devote funds to short-term objectives before turning your attention to long-term objectives. If at all possible, automate your savings contributions to maintain discipline and consistency in your saving practices.

To sum up, saving is an effective strategy for obtaining financial independence, stability, and peace of mind. Setting aside money for savings and understanding the difference between short- and long-term objectives will help you build a secure and productive financial future.

Chapter 4: Smart Investing Principles

Achieving financial independence and accumulating wealth requires investing. On the other hand, sound knowledge of investment vehicles, methods, and concepts is necessary for effective investing. We'll look at the principles of wise investing in this chapter, along with how to create an investment plan that fits your objectives and risk tolerance.

Comprehending Investment Instruments and Choices

It's important to comprehend the several investment vehicles and possibilities that are available to you before you jump into investing. The following list of typical investment vehicles includes their attributes:

1. Stocks: In addition to offering the possibility of dividends and capital growth, stocks also symbolise ownership in a company. You can take part in the expansion of particular companies by investing in individual stocks, but the

risk associated with this strategy is higher because of market volatility.

2. Bonds: To raise money, governments, towns, or businesses may issue bonds, which are debt securities. They offer a smaller potential return than stocks but a stable income stream in the form of interest payments. They are also typically regarded as safer than stocks.

3. Mutual funds: These investment vehicles combine the capital of several participants to purchase a variety of stocks, bonds, and other assets. In exchange for a fee, they provide expert management and diversity.

4.   Exchange-traded funds (ETFs): TRADING on stock exchanges like individual equities, ETFs are comparable to mutual funds. Due to their minimal expenses, tax efficiency, and flexibility in intraday trading, they are well-liked by many investors.

5. Real estate: Investing in real estate entails buying physical properties or real estate investment trusts (REITs), which are entities that hold and oversee properties that generate revenue. Potential benefits of real estate investing include diversification of portfolios, appreciation, and rental income.

6.   Alternative   investments: Cryptocurrencies, precious metals, hedge funds, commodities, and private equity are examples of alternative investments. These investments need considerable thought and research because they frequently have distinct risk-return profiles and may offer benefits for diversification.

Creating an Investment Plan That Takes Goals and Risk Tolerance into Account

Developing an investing strategy that fits your financial objectives, time horizon, and risk tolerance comes next after you have a solid understanding of the various investment alternatives. Here are some essential ideas to think about:

1. Clearly define your investment goals. Whether you want to save for retirement, pay for school, or become financially independent, decide what your goals are. Creating SMART (specific, measurable, achievable, relevant, and time-bound) goals will assist you in making more informed financial choices.

2. Determine your risk tolerance: Recognise the level of risk you can and will tolerate while making investments. Your risk tolerance is influenced by various factors, including age, investing

horizon, financial status, and temperament. Select investments based on your level of risk tolerance to prevent making rash decisions amid market turbulence.

3. Diversify your portfolio: To lower risk, diversification is a basic investing idea that calls for distributing your investments throughout a variety of industries, asset classes, and geographical areas. Long-term gains can be increased and losses during market downturns can be minimised with a well-diversified portfolio.

4. Retain a long-term outlook: Patience and discipline are necessary for successful investing. Instead of acting rashly in response to transient market swings, concentrate on your long-term investing objectives. Continue to make investments throughout market cycles, and periodically assess and adjust your portfolio as necessary.

5. Monitor and tweak your plan: Keep tabs on the performance of your investments and reassess your plan from time to time to make sure it still fits your objectives and risk tolerance. Adapt as needed to your changing financial

circumstances, the state of the market, and your investing goals.

To sum up, the first stages to wise investing are comprehending investment vehicles and possibilities and creating an investment plan that fits your objectives and risk tolerance. Your long-term financial success can be supported by a varied investment portfolio that you can create by adhering to these guidelines and maintaining discipline.

Chapter 5: Building Wealth Through Passive Income

One effective strategy for increasing wealth is passive income, which lets people make money with little continuing work or direct involvement. Passive income streams produce income continuously even when you're not actively working, in contrast to traditional types of income where you exchange time for money. This chapter will cover the idea of passive income, different opportunities and streams of passive income, and methods for developing and expanding passive income sources.

Investigating Prospects and Sources of Passive Income

There are several ways to generate passive income, and each has advantages and opportunities of its own. Consider the following typical passive income sources:

1. Rental income: One of the most common ways to generate passive income is to own rental properties and collect rent from renters. In addition to possible long-term gains and tax

advantages, real estate investments can offer consistent income flow.

2. Dividend-paying stocks: Purchasing dividend-paying stocks entitles you to recurring income in the form of dividends, which are normally given by publicly traded corporations on a quarterly or annual basis. For long-term investors, dividend stocks can be a dependable source of passive income with the potential for capital growth.

3. Interest-bearing investments: Interest payments are a passive source of income for interest-bearing investments including bonds, certificates of deposit

(CDs), and savings accounts. These investments provide stable and predictable income, notwithstanding the possibility of fluctuating interest rates.

4. Royalties: Payments obtained for the use of intellectual property include royalties from creative works like music, art, and books as well as patents, copyrights, and trademarks. For inventors and producers, royalties might offer passive income sources.

5. Peer-to-peer lending: Through these online platforms, people can lend money to one another in return for interest. Peer-to-peer lending is a way for

investors to diversify their investment portfolios and generate passive income.

6. Affiliate marketing: With affiliate marketing, you can recommend goods and services and get paid a commission for any purchases or recommendations that result from your advertising. Affiliate marketers that use websites, blogs, social media, and other platforms to promote items can generate passive revenue.

7. Digital products and online courses: Through royalties and recurrent sales, the creation and marketing of digital products such as software, e-books, and

online courses can result in passive income. Digital products don't require further work to sell again once they are generated.

Methods for Establishing and Expanding Passive Revenue Sources

Building passive income streams takes careful preparation, devotion, and constant work, even though it offers the possibility of financial freedom and flexibility. The following are some methods for developing and expanding sources of passive income:

1.   Determine your interests and strengths: To find passive income options that fit with your passions and talents, start by determining your hobbies, skills, and areas of competence. Select sources of income that you are willing to put in the time and effort to cultivate and that you find enjoyable.

2.   Make educational and training investments: Get the information, abilities, and instruction required to be successful in the passive income endeavours you have selected. To increase your proficiency and success rate, enrol in classes, go to workshops,

study books, and pick the brains of professionals.

3. Create several revenue streams: To lower risk and boost earning potential, diversify your passive income sources. Investigate several options to build a diverse portfolio of passive income streams rather than depending just on one.

4. Make use of technology and automation: Boost your passive income endeavours and streamline procedures by utilising software, technology, and automation solutions to automate tedious chores. Invest in infrastructure

and processes that will enable you to make money with little continuing work.

5. Constantly optimise and improve: To find opportunities for optimisation and improvement, analyse and evaluate your passive income streams on a regular basis. Try a variety of tactics, monitor your progress, and make any modifications to optimise your income.

In summary, accumulating money through passive income needs meticulous preparation, commitment, and continuous work. You can achieve financial freedom and design an abundant and prosperous life by investigating passive income streams and opportunities, determining your abilities and interests, and putting into practice efficient tactics for developing and expanding passive income sources.

Chapter 6: Real Estate Investment Strategies

Investing in real estate is a well-liked and proven method of accumulating wealth that has several advantages, such as the ability to generate passive income, diversify your portfolio, enjoy tax benefits, and possibly even appreciate in value. This chapter will cover the foundations of real estate investing, including various investment approaches, factors to take into account while choosing and managing properties, and advice for achieving success in the real estate market.

A Brief Overview of Real Estate Investing

Investing in real estate is buying, holding, and maintaining properties with the goal of increasing wealth and earning income. Real estate investing can be done in a number of ways, each with pros and downsides of its own:

1. Rental properties: One of the most popular types of real estate investing is the ownership of rental properties that are leased to tenants. Through rental revenue, the possibility of property

appreciation, and tax advantages like depreciation and mortgage interest deductions, rental properties can offer consistent cash flow.

2. Companies that own, manage, or finance income-producing real estate in a range of property sectors, such as residential, commercial, and industrial properties, are known as real estate investment trusts, or REITs. Purchasing through REITs offers liquidity and diversification while granting investors access to real estate markets without requiring them to hold physical properties directly.

3. Real estate crowdfunding: Through syndicated funds or pooled funds, individuals can invest in real estate projects or properties through platforms that facilitate real estate crowdfunding. Through crowdfunding, investors can diversify their holdings over a number of properties or projects and take advantage of real estate opportunities with lower capital requirements.

4. Fix-and-flip properties: Fix-and-flip investing is buying properties that are in need of repair or rehabilitation, then turning a profit by selling them. Even while fix-and-flip investments can be very profitable, in order to maximise

returns, thorough market analysis, refurbishment management, and sales timing are necessary.

5. Real estate development: This entails purchasing land, securing the required licences and permissions, and building or renovating properties that will be offered for sale or rental. Mixed-use complexes and industrial parks are examples of real estate development projects, as well as residential subdivisions and commercial buildings.

Attention to Detail in the Selection and Management of Properties

When choosing and maintaining properties, there are a number of elements that need to be carefully considered for real estate investing to be successful. The following are some important things to remember:

1. Location: Among the most crucial elements in real estate investing is location. Select real estate in sought-after areas with high demand, top-notch schools, convenient locations, and room to develop and appreciate in the future.

2. Property type: Take into account the kind of property that best fits your investing objectives, level of risk

tolerance, and level of experience. Single-family residences, multi-family dwellings, business structures, industrial warehouses, and undeveloped land are among the available options.

3. Financial analysis: Examine prospective properties' cash flow and possible return on investment (ROI) by conducting a detailed financial study. Take into account elements like the purchase price, operation costs, rental income, financing costs, vacancy rates, and possible appreciation.

4. Property condition: Evaluate the state of properties and note any maintenance

concerns, renovations, or repairs that are required. When assessing the entire investment potential and return on investment, take the cost of repairs and enhancements into account.

5. Property management: Choose between hiring a seasoned property management business or managing properties yourself to take care of upkeep, rent collecting, tenant relations, and day-to-day operations. To maximise rental income, cut costs, and maintain property value, effective property management is essential.

To sum up, investing in real estate presents a multitude of chances for accumulating money and attaining financial autonomy. Through a thorough understanding of real estate investing principles, investigation of various investment approaches, and meticulous evaluation of elements like property selection and management, investors may confidently traverse the real estate market and realise their financial objectives.

Chapter 7: Retirement Planning and Wealth Preservation

In order to provide long-term financial security and stability throughout the retirement years, retirement planning is a crucial component of financial management. Furthermore, wealth preservation techniques are necessary to protect accrued wealth and sustain long-term financial stability. We'll look at the value of retirement planning, money preservation techniques, and important factors to take into account to make sure you have a comfortable retirement in this chapter.

The Significance of Retirement Planning for Extended Financial Stability

Planning for retirement include establishing financial objectives, estimating retirement income requirements, and putting plans in place to reach those objectives. The following justifies the importance of retirement preparation for long-term financial security:

1. Replacing income from employment with other sources of income is the goal

of retirement planning. These sources of income include retirement savings, investments, pensions, and Social Security payments. People can make sure they have enough money in retirement to support the lifestyle they want by making advance plans.

2. Extended retirement periods: Life expectancy has considerably increased due to advancements in healthcare and medical technology. Retirement planning assists people in arranging their finances in order to pay for long-term care, healthcare, and other necessities as well as to prepare for a possibly lengthy retirement.

3. Protection against inflation: As inflation affects living standards and retirement savings, it gradually reduces the purchasing value of money. Investing in assets that give inflation-adjusted returns is one way to hedge against inflation and make sure retirement income keeps up with growing costs. Other tactics included in retirement planning are similar.

4. Social Security uncertainty: Despite being a useful retirement income source for many, Social Security's long-term viability is in doubt because of shifting demographics and budgetary constraints. Retirement planning assists people in

reducing their need on government aid by allowing them to augment their Social Security payments with additional sources of income and savings.

5. Lifestyle decisions: Retirement planning enables people to decide on a retirement lifestyle that includes where to live, when to retire, and how to divide their assets. People can afford to follow their passions, hobbies, and travel goals when they prepare ahead of time.

Wealth Preservation and Asset Protection Strategies

Strategies to safeguard accumulated assets, reduce taxes, and guarantee the long-term growth and sustainability of wealth are all part of wealth preservation. Here are a few crucial methods for protecting assets and preserving wealth:

1. Diversification: Spreading risk and reducing possible losses during market downturns can be achieved by diversifying investment portfolios across various asset classes, including stocks, bonds, real estate, and alternative assets. Over time, diversification can produce steady returns and aid in capital preservation.

2. Estate planning: Creating a detailed strategy for the transfer of wealth to heirs and beneficiaries is known as estate planning. People can make sure their assets are dispersed in accordance with their preferences, reduce estate taxes, and take care of their loved ones by using instruments like wills, trusts, and powers of attorney.

3. Asset protection vehicles can be used to protect assets from creditors, lawsuits, and other potential threats. Examples of asset protection vehicles are limited liability organisations (LLCs), trusts, and insurance policies. Asset protection plans

offer financial security and comfort against unanticipated obligations.

4. Tax-efficient investing: Tax liabilities can be reduced and after-tax returns can be improved by putting tax-efficient investment strategies into practice, such as employing tax-loss harvesting techniques and increasing contributions to tax-advantaged retirement plans (401(k), IRA, etc.). To protect money and get the best possible financial results, tax planning is crucial.

5. Long-term care planning: This entails getting ready for the possibility that you will require ongoing medical attention

and support as you age. People can safeguard their assets from the high costs of long-term care services and maintain financial security by looking into solutions including annuities, healthcare savings accounts, and long-term care insurance.

In summary, in order to ensure long-term financial security, stability, and peace of mind, retirement planning and wealth preservation are crucial elements of financial management. Through comprehending the significance of retirement planning, executing tactics to maintain wealth, and obtaining expert advice as required, people can accomplish their retirement objectives and relish a financially stable future.

Chapter 8: Continuous Learning and Financial Education

A lifetime path towards financial literacy, financial education equips people to manage their resources wisely, make wise financial decisions, and reach their financial objectives. This chapter will cover the value of financial literacy, methods for developing financial literacy, and resources for ongoing education and training in the field of personal finance.

Developing Financial Knowledge and Literacy

The capacity to comprehend and handle several facets of personal money, such as budgeting, saving, investing, borrowing, and retirement planning, is referred to as financial literacy. To successfully navigate intricate financial systems, stay clear of frequent hazards, and lay the groundwork for long-term financial stability, people must develop their financial literacy. The following are some methods for fostering financial literacy:

1. Begin with the fundamentals: Start by becoming familiar with the basic ideas of personal finance, such as debt

management, saving, and budgeting. Comprehending these fundamentals establishes the foundation for more sophisticated financial acumen and judgement.

2. Benefit from educational materials: To improve your financial literacy, examine a variety of educational resources, such as books, articles, podcasts, online courses, and workshops. Seek reliable information from financial advisors, instructors, and groups that promote financial literacy.

3. Remain informed: Keep up with news and events related to finance, the

economy, and current affairs that could affect your financial status. To keep informed and educated about financial matters, read reliable financial blogs and websites, participate in financial communities, and subscribe to financial magazines.

4. Seek expert counsel: If you're looking for individualised financial advice and guidance based on your unique needs and goals, you might choose to consult with licenced financial planners, advisors, or coaches. A financial expert may assist you in creating a thorough financial strategy, addressing particular

issues, and arriving at well-informed financial judgements.

5. Develop critical thinking abilities: Use your critical thinking abilities to assess financial data, goods, and services. When making financial decisions, be wary of claims of fast cures or get-rich-quick scams and do extensive research. Protecting oneself and your financial interests requires being able to tell the difference between trustworthy sources of information and financial frauds.

6. Learn from experience: Seize the chance to gain knowledge from your own financial achievements and failures.

Examine your previous financial choices, note where you could have done better, and use the knowledge you gained to inform your future financial planning and decision-making. For both financial success and personal development, ongoing introspection and learning are crucial.

Sources for Additional Education and Training

For those looking to increase their financial literacy, there is no shortage of information. The following resources are suggested for additional education and growth in the area of personal finance:

1. literature: Examine a wide range of personal financial literature on subjects like wealth creation, investing, retirement planning, and budgeting. Seek for best-selling books written by well-known financial authorities and instructors.

2. Online courses: Take advantage of the educational opportunities provided by respectable colleges, universities, and financial institutions by enrolling in online courses. You can learn at your own pace and convenience with the help of numerous online platforms that provide courses on a variety of personal finance-related topics.

3. Podcasts: Take in financial podcasts presented by thought leaders, financial advisors, and industry professionals. Podcasts are an easily accessible and practical learning resource that offer insightful analysis, practical advice, and well-thought-out tactics on a variety of financial subjects.

4. Websites and blogs: Look through financial blogs and websites that provide you with tools, calculators, guidelines, and educational materials to help you become more financially literate and make wise decisions. Seek out websites connected to reputable banks,

governmental bodies, and charitable outfits.

5. Workshops and seminars: Participate in financial webinars, workshops, and seminars that are presented by educational institutions, community organisations, and financial specialists. These gatherings offer chances to talk with personal finance enthusiasts, get advice from professionals, and pose questions.

6. Financial literacy efforts and programmes: Take part in the financial literacy campaigns and programmes that local, state, and federal governments are

offering. These initiatives frequently include workshops, instructional materials, and free or inexpensive tools to support people in developing their financial literacy.

Through the use of these resources and a dedication to ongoing education and growth, people can improve their financial literacy, make wise financial decisions, and eventually attain financial success and freedom.

Chapter 9: Overcoming Financial Obstacles

Unexpected financial setbacks can occur, posing difficulties that could impede the path to financial independence. This section will discuss frequent financial difficulties that people may encounter as well as methods for getting out of debt and increasing one's financial resilience.

Identifying and Addressing Common Financial Challenges

1. Income instability: It might be difficult to properly budget and plan for future expenses when income levels fluctuate. People whose income fluctuates or is seasonal may find it difficult to pay for necessities during hard times. Consider diversifying your sources of income, setting up an emergency fund to protect against market changes, and looking for other sources of income in order to manage income instability.

2. High debt levels: Carrying a lot of debt might make it hard for a person to stay stable financially and reach their goals. Credit card debt, student loans, mortgages, and personal loans are

examples of common debt categories. Use a debt repayment plan, such the debt avalanche or snowball method, to prioritise repaying debt in order to reduce high debt levels. Investigate your alternatives for debt consolidation or refinancing as well in order to reduce interest rates and simplify payments.

3. Lack of savings: People who don't have enough savings may be more susceptible to unforeseen costs and financial emergencies. Many people find it difficult to save because of conflicting financial priorities, low incomes, or poor budgeting practices. Setting aside a portion of your monthly income and

creating a realistic savings goal are the first steps in building savings. To guarantee regularity, think about automating your savings contributions. To maximise the rewards on your funds, look into high-yield savings accounts or investment opportunities.

4. Financial illiteracy: People who lack basic financial knowledge and abilities may find it more difficult to manage their money wisely and make wise financial decisions. A lack of knowledge of fundamental financial ideas, inadequate money management techniques, or vulnerability to financial frauds and predatory tactics are some examples of

financial illiteracy. Give financial education first priority and look for tools to help you become more financially literate in order to combat financial illiteracy. Utilise seminars, internet resources, and educational opportunities to expand your financial literacy and form wise financial practices.

5. Unexpected expenses: Unexpected costs can put a strain on limited resources and cause financial instability. Examples of these costs include car repairs, home maintenance, and medical emergencies. In the absence of sufficient emergency reserves or a safety net, people could have to borrow money at

exorbitant interest rates or spend all of their resources to fund unforeseen expenses. Create a separate fund for irregular or periodic expenses and develop an emergency reserve equivalent to three to six months' worth of living expenses to prepare for unforeseen expenses. Examine insurance policies to be sure you are adequately covered in case of unforeseen circumstances, and look into opportunities for extra coverage or riders if necessary.

Strategies for Overcoming Debt and Building Financial Resilience

1. Adopt a sensible spending plan: Create a thorough budget that takes into consideration all sources of income and outlays, such as debt repayment, necessities for a healthy lifestyle, and discretionary expenditure. Make paying off debt your top priority by setting aside a certain percentage of your monthly income for this purpose and reducing non-essential spending to free up extra cash.

2. Negotiate with creditors: If you're having trouble making your debt payments, think about getting in touch with your creditors to work out better terms for repayment, such longer

payback terms, reduced interest rates, or debt settlement agreements. When borrowers are having financial difficulties, many creditors are eager to collaborate with them to create win-win solutions.

3. Investigate debt consolidation: You can simplify debt repayment and save interest expenses overall by combining high-interest debt into a single, lower-interest loan. Examine your alternatives for combining debt, including home equity loans, personal loans, and credit card balance transfers. Weigh terms and costs to determine which option is best for you.

4. Seek expert assistance: If you're having trouble managing your money or are overburdened with debt, you might want to consult a financial advisor, debt relief company, or credit counsellor. These experts may offer you individualised advice and assistance to help you create a plan for paying off debt, hone your budgeting abilities, and take back control of your finances.

5. Keep your long-term financial goals in mind: Paying off debt may need you to make some short-term sacrifices, but it's important to stay motivated and focused on your long-term objectives. Imagine the advantages of being debt-free,

including more financial flexibility, less stress, and the capacity to accumulate money and realise your aspirations. Remain dedicated to your financial objectives and acknowledge your progress to sustain drive and inspiration.

Individuals can take charge of their finances, achieve debt freedom, and pave the path towards long-term financial success and security by recognising and addressing common financial challenges as well as putting strategies for overcoming debt and building financial resilience into practice.

Conclusion

In summary, obtaining financial independence needs commitment, self-control, and thoughtful preparation. We have covered a variety of financial techniques in this book with the intention of empowering readers to take charge of their money, accumulate wealth, and meet their long-term financial objectives. Let's review some of the most important financial techniques that were covered and inspire you to move towards financial independence.

Summary of Crucial Financial Techniques for Attaining Financial Independence

1. Foundations of Financial Freedom: First, we established what financial freedom is and what our individual financial objectives are. A strong basis for financial planning and decision-making is provided by realising the significance of financial independence and setting specific goals.

2. Budgeting for Success: Tracking income, controlling spending, and reaching financial stability all depend on the creation and upkeep of a personal

budget. People can maximise their savings potential and optimise their budgeting efforts by setting financial goals, minimising discretionary spending, and prioritising necessities.

3. The Power of Saving: Over time, savings may help you accumulate money, fund your ambitions, and act as a safety net in case of emergencies. It is an essential part of being financially successful. A proactive approach to saving can help people create sound financial practices and work towards their long-term financial goals.

4. Wise Investing Principles: Compared to saving alone, investing provides a quicker path to financial goals and wealth growth. People may make educated investment decisions and maximise their investment returns by learning about investment options, creating a diversified investment strategy, and keeping up with market developments.

5. Building Wealth With Passive Income: Passive income streams are a further source of income that may be used to augment earned income and hasten the creation of wealth. People can create passive income and become financially independent by looking at passive

income opportunities like rental properties, dividend-paying stocks, or web enterprises.

6. Real Estate Investment Strategies: Diversifying investment portfolios, creating rental income, and accumulating wealth are all made possible by real estate investing. People can reap the potential rewards of real estate investing by studying about investment strategies, analysing potential properties, and comprehending market dynamics.

7. Wealth Preservation and Retirement Planning: To provide long-term financial security and protect resources for future

generations, retirement planning is crucial. People may live well in retirement and leave a legacy for their loved ones by creating a thorough retirement plan, investigating retirement savings choices, and putting wealth preservation techniques into practise.

8. Financial Education and Continuous Learning: Making wise financial decisions and adjusting to shifting market conditions depend on developing one's financial literacy and remaining current on personal finance issues. People can increase their financial literacy and well-being by investing in financial education, looking for reliable

sources, and keeping up with news and trends in the financial world.

9. Overcoming Financial difficulties: Despite being an unavoidable part of the path to financial independence, financial difficulties can be surmounted with tenacity and resolve. People can overcome financial setbacks and continue on their path to reaching their financial objectives by recognising typical financial obstacles, putting debt reduction and financial resilience methods into practice, and getting professional help when necessary.

Inspiration to Act and Aim for Financial Objectives

As we come to the end of our investigation on financial independence tactics, I urge you to act and give your financial objectives top priority. Recall that achieving financial freedom requires commitment to strong financial principles, perseverance, and dedication. Remember that every step you take towards reaching financial freedom and building the life you want, regardless of where you are in your financial path or how far you want to go. Remain determined and focused, and never undervalue the influence that your financial choices will have on your future.

I'll end by wishing you well as you go towards financial independence. I hope you make sensible financial decisions, get past any challenges you face, and reap the benefits of financial independence for many years to come.